The TRUSTED BANKER's

FINANCIAL FITNESS PLANNER

Challenging 1 Million People To Become **Bankable**

Written by: LYSA BRADFORD-DAVIS

The Trusted Banker's
Financial Fitness Challenge

Published by **Lysa Bradford Davis**
The Trusted Banker is a trademark and may not be used without written permission.
www.thetrustedbanker.com

Content Development and Editing
Lysa Bradford Davis

Design and Layout
Lysa Bradford Davis

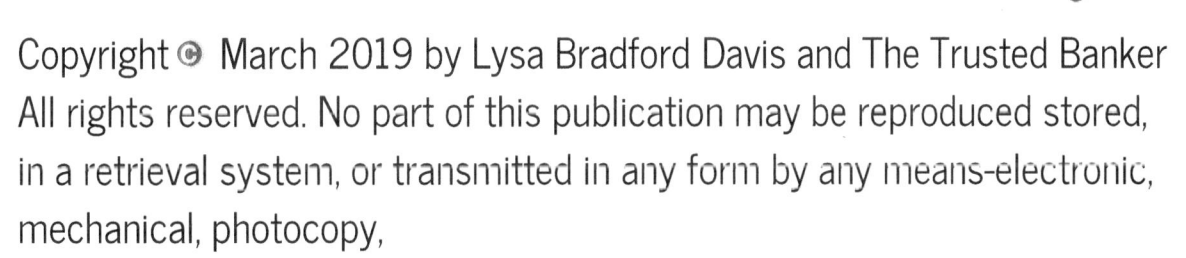

Copyright © March 2019 by Lysa Bradford Davis and The Trusted Banker
All rights reserved. No part of this publication may be reproduced stored, in a retrieval system, or transmitted in any form by any means-electronic, mechanical, photocopy,
recording, or otherwise-except for brief quotations in critical reviews or articles, without the prior permission of the publisher, except as provided by US copyright law.
Third Edition Published 2020

Thank you to my daughters Symone and Brittanie
Because of you, I am.
I Love You,
Momma

9781716825873

LET'S GET FINANCIALLY FIT

THE TRUSTED BANKER'S FINANCIAL FITNESS DAILY PLANNER

TABLE OF CONTENTS

- Congratulations
- Things You Will Need
- Daily Tasks
- Your Monthly Budget
- Spending Habits
- Goals Selection
- Monthly Goals
- Yearly Goals
- Long Term Goals
- Spending Logs
- Daily Planner

The Trusted Banker

LET'S GET FINANCIALLY FIT

THE TRUSTED BANKER'S FINANCIAL FITNESS DAILY PLANNER

Congratulations!

Congratulations on taking the first step to becoming a more financially fit you! Give yourself a pat on the back. This is going to be a challenging but rewarding journey. I've spent the past 20 years helping people across America learn how to successfully manage their money by developing a customized financial management plan that put into a book that also serves as a daily planner. You will learn how to:

- Create a Personal Budget
- Manage Your Time
- Monitor and Manage your Credit
- Create a Debt Dissolution Plan
- Improve and Increase Your FICO Score

And Much, Much More!

The Trusted Banker

LET'S GET FINANCIALLY FIT

THE TRUSTED BANKER
FINANCIAL FITNESS DAILY PLANNER

This planner was designed with you in mind. We introduce budgeting techniques that you can easily incorporate into your everyday life, review basic money management skills and help you develop future goals to increase your revenue generating systems to increase personal wealth. The Financially Fit Daily Planner was designed to by used every 90 days. Instilling new habits until they become a part of your daily life. Every time you complete the 90 days, you learn something new.

So if you make a mistake, don't worry, just keep going. You will have a chance to make up for it during your next 90 days.

Just don't quit.

Keep Going.

The Trusted Banker

THINGS YOU WILL NEED

THE TRUSTED BANKER'S FINANCIAL FITNESS DAILY PLANNER

Preparation is the name of the game! In addition to your daily planner, here is a list of some items you will need as you work toward "Financial Fitness"

- Paper Clips
- 6 Envelopes
- 1 Large Jar
- Access to a Laptop
- Paper and Pencil
- Access to Google Play or The App Store
- Calculator

The Trusted Banker

DAILY TASKS

THE TRUSTED BANKER'S
FINANCIAL FITNESS DAILY PLANNER

The purpose of this planner is to hold you accountable and keep you on task as you build new habits for money management and financial fitness.

Everyday you will have a 'Daily Task' to complete. These daily tasks are designed to take less than 10 minutes per day, while teaching critical money management techniques. Each daily task is a building block. If you complete all of the daily tasks, at the end of 90 days you will have built a strong foundation that will carry you through to financial fitness.

In addition to your daily tasks, you will have a daily spending log to keep a record of your daily expenditures.

The Trusted Banker

DAILY TASKS

THE TRUSTED BANKER'S FINANCIAL FITNESS DAILY PLANNER

Getting financially fit will require being transparent and honest with yourself about your money management habits.

Sometimes you will feel uncomfortable.

It's okay.

Anyone that has changed for the better will tell you that the journey is not always pleasant, but the results are worth it.

The **"Savings Challenge"**, if done correctly, will help you save over $450.00 each month.

That's over $1300.00 in 90 days!

This money can be used to pay off a bill, plan a vacation or invest in something you've always wanted. The choice is yours. The saving habits you learn can lead to saving almost $5000 a year or $20,000 in 4 years.

Think about what you can do with that amount of savings!

The Trusted Banker

YOUR MONTHLY BUDGET

THE TRUSTED BANKER'S
FINANCIAL FITNESS DAILY PLANNER

Included with this challenge is a monthly budget.

Each month you have "Free Days" to give you extra time to work on your monthly budget. Your monthly budget is important, because it's a written record of your monthly income, monthly bills and expenses.

It is important to be completely honest with yourself and record actual numbers.

Completing your monthly budget helps you identify where you are spending your money and if there is an opportunity to cut back or decrease spending.

Make sure you record your weekly spending log totals on your budget.

The goal is to increase your savings, decrease your debt & get financially fit.

The Trusted Banker

SPENDING HABITS

THE TRUSTED BANKER'S FINANCIAL FITNESS DAILY PLANNER

Changing our spending habits is not easy. I'm talking about making long term changes. Not short term, starting over again change that is over before it begins.

Long term change of behavior is one of the hardest things any of us will ever try to do. Let me share an excerpt from an article written by **David DiSalvo**, for Psychology Today.(7/22/17)

"Change is never just one thing; it's a lot of connected things, and sustained change doesn't happen without a process that considers all of the pieces. It's easy to fool ourselves into believing that it should be so much simpler, but nothing about behavior change is simple. It's a tough, process-oriented challenge to move the needle even a little."

So be patient and consistent, and allow it to happen.

The Trusted Banker

SETTING GOALS

THE TRUSTED BANKER'S FINANCIAL FITNESS DAILY PLANNER

Setting small obtainable goals that you can complete over time add up to cumulative change.

When you set goals you inspire self improvement while giving yourself something to work towards. Everyone needs an objective. Something to strive for, something to hope and dream about. Setting goals for yourself is a way to fuel your ambition.

In Your Financial Fitness Planner You Will Learn

How to set one month goals.

How to set one year goals.

How to set long term goals.

MONTHLY GOALS

THE TRUSTED BANKER'S
FINANCIAL FITNESS DAILY PLANNER

Monthly goals are short term goals that should be simple and achievable to keep you motivated. Creating a continuous streak of short term wins proves that you are able to achieve anything you set your mind to.

What's the easiest way to eat an elephant?

One bite at a time.

Below is a list of short term goals you can use for your "Daily Task on Day 3", or you can create your own.

- Open a savings account
- Read a newspaper article in the finance section
- Read a stock market article: Ex. Marketwatch
- Take a free online course
- Read a book
- Talk about your Financial Fitness journey

The Trusted Banker

ONE YEAR GOALS

THE TRUSTED BANKER'S FINANCIAL FITNESS DAILY PLANNER

Yearly goals should be something that you can achieve using your monthly goals as building blocks. For example, if you have a monthly goal of reading the stock market, then your "One Year Goal" could be something like.......... **opening an investment account to buy stocks.** Your one year goal will help you maintain your vision for your future. There are different types of long term goals. Some can be achieved in 12 months, like losing weight, and some can be achieved in several years, like earning a degree. Setting yearly goals, gives you benchmarks on your way to bigger and better. **A few examples of "One Year Goals"**

- Open an investment account
- Enroll in a college course
- Open a Christmas saving account
- Pay off one large bill

The Trusted Banker

LONG TERM GOALS

THE TRUSTED BANKER'S FINANCIAL FITNESS DAILY PLANNER

Long term goals are something that you want to achieve further into the future. The secret to accomplishing your long term goals, is to build up to final goal over time. Stack smaller goals like building blocks, when you stack that last block.....Goal Accomplished!

> *Your monthly goals are building your foundation, exchanging bad habits for good. Yearly goals are the enforcement, the structure beams providing the framework for the "New You"*

Your Long Term Goals is your reward after all of your hard work. Your ultimate achievement that you can enjoy for the rest of your life. A sample list of "Long Term Goals" below:

- Purchase a new house
- Buy or pay off a new car
- Start a business
- Get your degree

The Trusted Banker

SPENDING LOGS

THE TRUSTED BANKER'S FINANCIAL FITNESS DAILY PLANNER

Logging your daily spending is an important exercise to stay conscious of the way you manage your money. It will be painful. I know firsthand. Years ago I did this and I was surprised at how much money I spent weekly. I was able to eliminate some expenses and start saving more money.

> *It won't be easy.*
> *But it is possible.*
> *Stick with it.*

An easy way to maintain your spending log is to ask for a receipt everywhere you go. Either take a picture of the receipt with your cell phone, or carry a small envelope or Ziploc bag to put the receipts in as soon as you get them. Every night, block off 15 minutes to record your spending on the correct day of the week.

BANKABLE SCHEDULE

DAY 1

DAILY TASKS:
VIEW BANK ACCOUNTS

- Review your Bank Accounts and write down your available balance in each account. You should always be aware of how much money is in your accounts.
- Complete your daily expense log
- Put $1.00 in your challenge envelope

DAILY EXPENSES:

FOOD

TRANSPORTATION

ENTERTAINMENT

GROCERIES

SHOPPING

OTHER

IMPORTANT NOTES:

BANKABLE SCHEDULE

Day 2

DAILY TASKS: CREATE ENVELOPE FOR PREVIOUS MONTH

- Collect all receipts from previous month and put them in an envelope. Label the front of the envelope with the Month and Year to easily identify.
- Complete your daily expense log.
- Put $2 in your challenge envelope.

DAILY EXPENSES:

FOOD

TRANSPORTATION

ENTERTAINMENT

GROCERIES

SHOPPING

OTHER

IMPORTANT NOTES:

BANKABLE SCHEDULE

DAY 3

DAILY TASKS:
MONTHLY GOALS

- Write down your goal for the month. You can select one from the choices on the monthly goal sheet, or create your own.
- Complete your daily expense log.
- Put $3 in your challenge envelope.

DAILY EXPENSES:

FOOD
_____

TRANSPORTATION
_____

ENTERTAINMENT
_____

GROCERIES
_____

SHOPPING
_____

OTHER
_____

IMPORTANT NOTES:

_____

_____

_____

_____

BANKABLE SCHEDULE

Day 4

DAILY TASKS:
COLLECT SPARE CHANGE

- Empty the spare change out of your pockets, purse, car and coats. Think of other places you may have spare change. Gather it and put it in a jar. Label the jar "My Savings Jar"
- Complete your daily expense log.
- Put $4 in your challenge envelope.

DAILY EXPENSES:

FOOD

TRANSPORTATION

ENTERTAINMENT

GROCERIES

SHOPPING

OTHER

IMPORTANT NOTES:

BANKABLE SCHEDULE

DAY 5

DAILY TASKS:
YOUR CREDIT REPORT

- Pull your free credit report from the website: www.annualcreditreport.com
-
- Complete your daily expense log.
- Put $5 in your challenge envelope.

DAILY EXPENSES:

FOOD

TRANSPORTATION

ENTERTAINMENT

GROCERIES

SHOPPING

OTHER

IMPORTANT NOTES:

BANKABLE SCHEDULE

Day 6

DAILY TASKS:
WEEKLY RECEIPTS

- Gather all your receipts from the week. Stack them by category (gas, food, shopping, dining, misc) and paper clip them together and place them in the monthly envelope.
- Complete your daily expense log.
- Put $6 in your challenge envelope.

DAILY EXPENSES:

FOOD

TRANSPORTATION

ENTERTAINMENT

GROCERIES

SHOPPING

OTHER

IMPORTANT NOTES:

BANKABLE SCHEDULE

DAY 7

DAILY TASKS:
TOTAL SPENDING LOGS

- Total your spending logs from the week and list the total on your master budget in the area labeled "Weekly Spending Log."
- This is week 1.
- Complete your daily expense log.
- Put $7 in your challenge envelope.

DAILY EXPENSES:

FOOD

TRANSPORTATION

ENTERTAINMENT

GROCERIES

SHOPPING

OTHER

IMPORTANT NOTES:

BANKABLE SCHEDULE

Day 8

DAILY TASKS:
TRY MONTHLY AUTOPAY

- Switch one monthly bill to auto-pay. Something small and affordable. Choose the monthly date you want the payment deducted, notate it on you calendar.
- Complete daily expense log.
- Put $8 in your challenge envelope

DAILY EXPENSES:

FOOD

TRANSPORTATION

ENTERTAINMENT

GROCERIES

SHOPPING

OTHER

IMPORTANT NOTES:

BANKABLE SCHEDULE

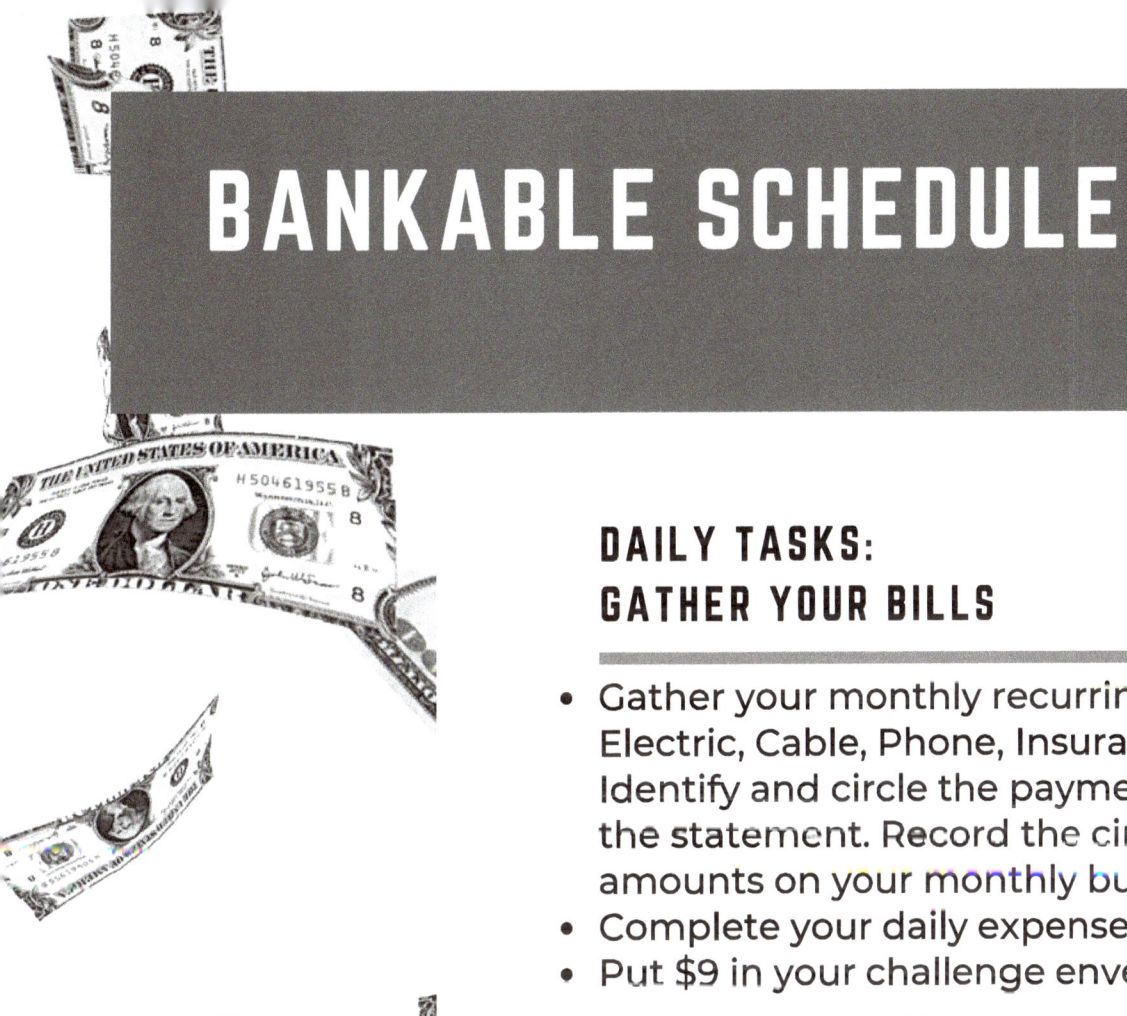

DAY 9

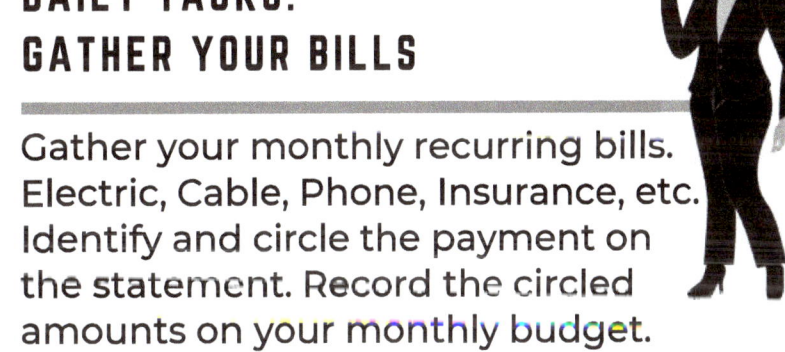

DAILY TASKS:
GATHER YOUR BILLS

- Gather your monthly recurring bills. Electric, Cable, Phone, Insurance, etc. Identify and circle the payment on the statement. Record the circled amounts on your monthly budget.
- Complete your daily expense log.
- Put $9 in your challenge envelope.

DAILY EXPENSES:

FOOD

TRANSPORTATION

ENTERTAINMENT

GROCERIES

SHOPPING

OTHER

IMPORTANT NOTES:

BANKABLE SCHEDULE

DAY 10

DAILY TASKS:
ONE YEAR GOAL

- Write down your one year goal somewhere you will see it. You can select one from the choices provided on the yearly goal sheet or create your own.
- Complete your daily expense log.
- Put $10 in your challenge envelope.

DAILY EXPENSES:

FOOD

TRANSPORTATION

ENTERTAINMENT

GROCERIES

SHOPPING

OTHER

IMPORTANT NOTES:

BANKABLE SCHEDULE

DAY 11

DAILY TASKS: FREE DAY!!!

- Complete your daily expense log.
- Put $11 in your challenge envelope.

DAILY EXPENSES:

FOOD

TRANSPORTATION

ENTERTAINMENT

GROCERIES

SHOPPING

OTHER

IMPORTANT NOTES:

BANKABLE SCHEDULE

DAY 12

DAILY TASKS:
READ YOUR CREDIT REPORT

- Read your free credit report. Verify your name, address, date of birth and social security number are accurate and spelled correctly.
- Complete your daily expense log.
- Put $12 in your challenge envelope.

DAILY EXPENSES:

FOOD
_____

TRANSPORTATION
_____

ENTERTAINMENT
_____

GROCERIES
_____

SHOPPING
_____

OTHER
_____

IMPORTANT NOTES:
_____
_____
_____
_____

BANKABLE SCHEDULE

DAY 13

DAILY TASKS:
GATHER YOUR RECEIPTS

- Categorize all your receipts for the week (gas, food, shopping, dining, misc.) paper clip them together to place in your monthly envelope.
- Complete your daily expense log.
- Put $13 in your challenge envelope.

DAILY EXPENSES:

FOOD

TRANSPORTATION

ENTERTAINMENT

GROCERIES

SHOPPING

OTHER

IMPORTANT NOTES:

BANKABLE SCHEDULE

DAY 14

DAILY TASKS:
TOTAL SPENDING LOGS

- Total your spending logs from the week and list the total on your master budget in the area labeled "Weekly Spending Log."
- This is week 2.
- Complete your daily expense log.
- Put $14 in your challenge envelope.

DAILY EXPENSES:

FOOD

TRANSPORTATION

ENTERTAINMENT

GROCERIES

SHOPPING

OTHER

IMPORTANT NOTES:

BANKABLE SCHEDULE

DAY 15

DAILY TASKS:
HALF WAY POINT

- Halfway into the month, take a look at available cash in your bank account. Think about how much income you will receive for the remainder of the month. Did you budget correctly?
- Complete daily expense log.
- Put $15 in your challenge envelope.

DAILY EXPENSES:

FOOD

TRANSPORTATION

ENTERTAINMENT

GROCERIES

SHOPPING

OTHER

IMPORTANT NOTES:

BANKABLE SCHEDULE

DAY 16

DAILY TASKS:
REDUCE MONTHLY DEBT

- Choose one monthly recurring bill. Create a strategy to reduce the debt. What can you go without? Netflix, Cellphone, Apple Music etc.
- Complete your daily expense log.
- Put $16 in your challenge envelope.

DAILY EXPENSES:

FOOD

TRANSPORTATION

ENTERTAINMENT

GROCERIES

SHOPPING

OTHER

IMPORTANT NOTES:

BANKABLE SCHEDULE

Day 17

DAILY TASKS:
LONG TERM GOAL

- Write down a long term goal. You can select one from the long term goal sheet or create your own.
- Complete daily expense log.
- Put $17 in your challenge envelope.

DAILY EXPENSES:

FOOD

TRANSPORTATION

ENTERTAINMENT

GROCERIES

SHOPPING

OTHER

IMPORTANT NOTES:

BANKABLE SCHEDULE

DAY 18

DAILY TASKS:
GATHER SPARE CHANGE

- Empty the spare change out of your pockets, purse, car and coats. Think of other places you may have spare change. Gather it and put it in a jar. Label the jar "My Savings Jar"
- Complete your daily expense log.
- Put 18 in your challenge envelope.

DAILY EXPENSES:

FOOD

TRANSPORTATION

ENTERTAINMENT

GROCERIES

SHOPPING

OTHER

IMPORTANT NOTES:

BANKABLE SCHEDULE

Day 19

DAILY TASKS:
DOCUMENT CREDIT REPORT

- On a piece of paper write down your collections, charge-offs, judgements, etc. listed on the credit report. In a separate column write down the monthly payments.
- Complete your daily expense log.
- Put $19 in your challenge envelope.

DAILY EXPENSES:

FOOD

TRANSPORTATION

ENTERTAINMENT

GROCERIES

SHOPPING

OTHER

IMPORTANT NOTES:

BANKABLE SCHEDULE

DAY 20

DAILY TASKS:
GATHER YOUR RECEIPTS

- Categorize all your receipts for the week (gas, food, shopping, dining, misc.) paper clip them together to place in your monthly envelope.
- Complete your daily expense log.
- Put $20 in your challenge envelope.

DAILY EXPENSES:

FOOD

TRANSPORTATION

ENTERTAINMENT

GROCERIES

SHOPPING

OTHER

IMPORTANT NOTES:

BANKABLE SCHEDULE

Day 21

DAILY TASKS:
TOTAL SPENDING LOGS

- Total your spending logs from the week and list the total on your master budget in the area labeled "Weekly Spending Log."
- This is week 3.
- Complete your daily expense log.
- Put $21 in your challenge envelope.

DAILY EXPENSES:

FOOD

TRANSPORTATION

ENTERTAINMENT

GROCERIES

SHOPPING

OTHER

IMPORTANT NOTES:

BANKABLE SCHEDULE

DAY 22

DAILY TASKS:
REVIEW BANK STATEMENT

- Review your bank statement. On your master budget, write down the date your monthly recurring bills are deducted from your account.
- Complete your daily expense log.
- Put $22 in your challenge envelope.

DAILY EXPENSES:

FOOD

TRANSPORTATION

ENTERTAINMENT

GROCERIES

SHOPPING

OTHER

IMPORTANT NOTES:

BANKABLE SCHEDULE

DAY 23

DAILY TASKS:
REDUCE MONTHLY DEBT

- Call the selected monthly from day 16. Ask if they have any specials to lower your bill. If not, tell them you are shopping other providers for the best rate.
- Complete your daily expense log.
- Put $23 in your challenge envelope.

DAILY EXPENSES:

FOOD

TRANSPORTATION

ENTERTAINMENT

GROCERIES

SHOPPING

OTHER

IMPORTANT NOTES:

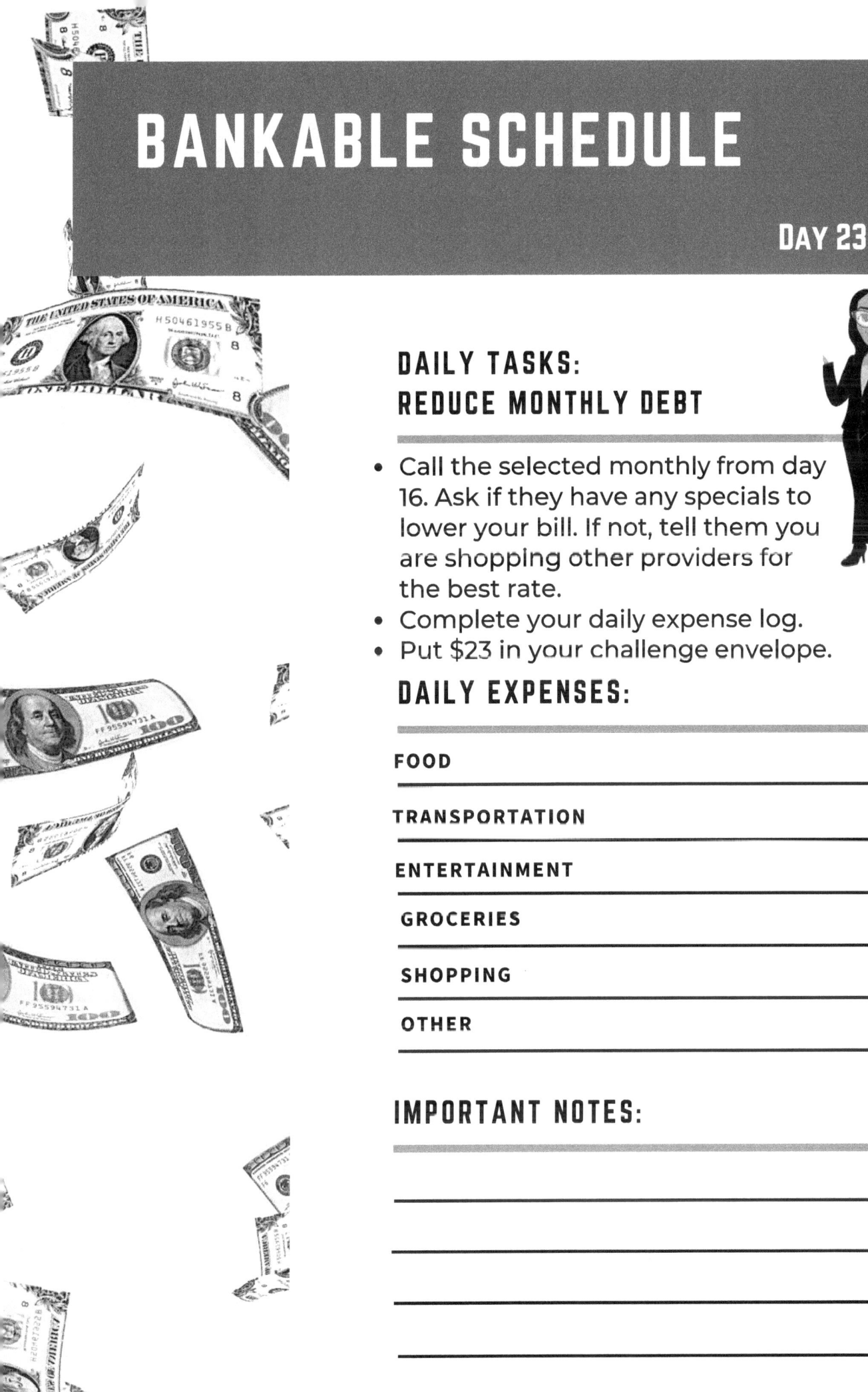

BANKABLE SCHEDULE

DAY 24

DAILY TASKS:
CALL COLLECTION ACCOUNTS

- Call and verify the collection is still active. Schedule a future date to call back and make payment arrangements. Stick to the plan.
- Complete your daily expense log.
- Put $24 in your challenge envelope.

DAILY EXPENSES:

FOOD

TRANSPORTATION

ENTERTAINMENT

GROCERIES

SHOPPING

OTHER

IMPORTANT NOTES:

BANKABLE SCHEDULE

DAY 25

DAILY TASKS: FREE DAY!!!

- Complete your daily expense log.
- Put $25 in your challenge envelope.

DAILY EXPENSES:

FOOD

TRANSPORTATION

ENTERTAINMENT

GROCERIES

SHOPPING

OTHER

IMPORTANT NOTES:

BANKABLE SCHEDULE

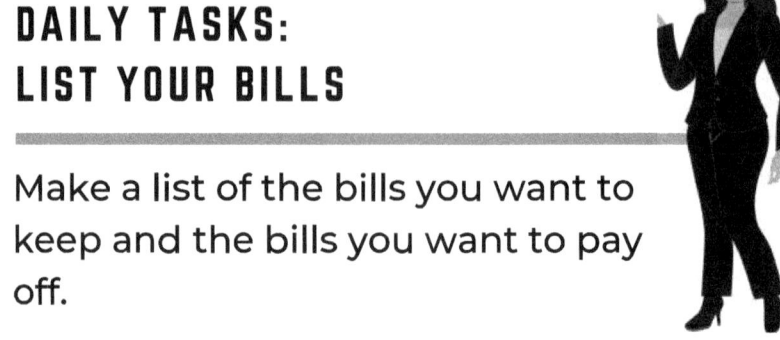

DAY 26

DAILY TASKS:
LIST YOUR BILLS

- Make a list of the bills you want to keep and the bills you want to pay off.

- Complete your daily expense log.
- Put $26 in your challenge envelope.

DAILY EXPENSES:

FOOD
___

TRANSPORTATION
___

ENTERTAINMENT
___

GROCERIES
___

SHOPPING
___

OTHER
___

IMPORTANT NOTES:

BANKABLE SCHEDULE

DAY 27

DAILY TASKS:
GATHER YOUR RECEIPTS

- Categorize all your receipts for the week (gas, food, shopping, dining, misc.) paper clip them together to place in your monthly envelope.
- Complete your daily expense log.
- Put $27 in your challenge envelope.

DAILY EXPENSES:

FOOD
_____

TRANSPORTATION
_____

ENTERTAINMENT
_____

GROCERIES
_____

SHOPPING
_____

OTHER
_____

IMPORTANT NOTES:
_____
_____
_____
_____
_____

BANKABLE SCHEDULE

DAY 28

DAILY TASKS:
TOTAL SPENDING LOGS

- Total your spending logs from the week and list the total on your master budget in the area labeled "Weekly Spending Log."
- This is week 4.
- Complete your daily expense log.
- Put $28 in your challenge envelope.

DAILY EXPENSES:

FOOD

TRANSPORTATION

ENTERTAINMENT

GROCERIES

SHOPPING

OTHER

IMPORTANT NOTES:

BANKABLE SCHEDULE

DAY 29

DAILY TASKS:
MAKE ADDITIONAL INCOME

- Identify ways you can make additional income. What are your hobbies? What do you like to do and what are you good at? What is your passion?
- Complete your daily expense log.
- Put $29 in your challenge envelope

DAILY EXPENSES:

FOOD

TRANSPORTATION

ENTERTAINMENT

GROCERIES

SHOPPING

OTHER

IMPORTANT NOTES:

BANKABLE SCHEDULE

DAY 30

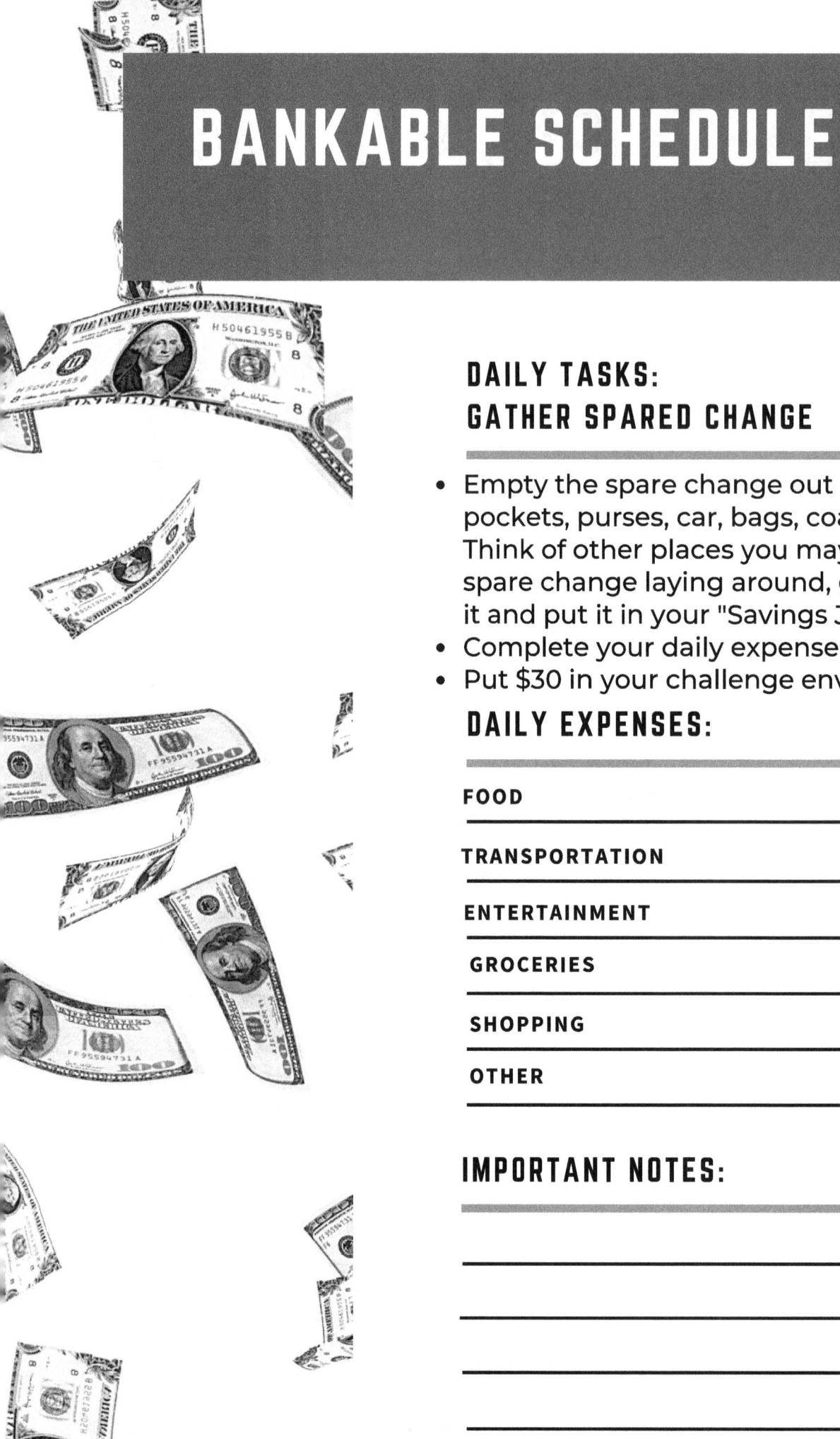

DAILY TASKS:
GATHER SPARED CHANGE

- Empty the spare change out of your pockets, purses, car, bags, coats. Think of other places you may have spare change laying around, gather it and put it in your "Savings Jar".
- Complete your daily expense log.
- Put $30 in your challenge envelope.

DAILY EXPENSES:

FOOD

TRANSPORTATION

ENTERTAINMENT

GROCERIES

SHOPPING

OTHER

IMPORTANT NOTES:

BANKABLE SCHEDULE

DAY 31

DAILY TASKS: FREE DAY!!!

- Complete your daily expense log.
- Put $31 in your challenge envelope.

DAILY EXPENSES:

FOOD

TRANSPORTATION

ENTERTAINMENT

GROCERIES

SHOPPING

OTHER

IMPORTANT NOTES:

_____ , 20 ___
month   day   year

MY DAILY PLANNER

THINGS TO DO

MY CONTACT LOG

REMINDERS & NOTES

The Trusted Banker

WEEKLY MONEY LOGS

MONDAY

TUESDAY

WEDNESDAY

THURSDAY

FRIDAY

SATURDAY

NOTES

The Trusted Banker

Bankable Planner
Short Term Goal Planner

SHORT TERM GOALS

Short Term Goals I'm Interested In

- [ ] _____
- [ ] _____
- [ ] _____
- [ ] _____
- [ ] _____
- [ ] _____
- [ ] _____

Notes to Self

_____

_____

_____

_____

_____

_____

Bankable Planner
Yearly Goal Planner

YEARLY GOALS

Yearly Goals I'm Interested In

- [ ] _____
- [ ] _____
- [ ] _____
- [ ] _____
- [ ] _____
- [ ] _____
- [ ] _____

Notes to Self

_____

_____

_____

_____

_____

BANKABLE PLANNER
LONG TERM GOAL PLANNER

LONG TERM GOALS

LONG TERM GOALS I'M INTERESTED IN

- ☐ _____
- ☐ _____
- ☐ _____
- ☐ _____
- ☐ _____
- ☐ _____
- ☐ _____

NOTES TO SELF

_____
_____
_____
_____
_____
_____

The Trusted Banker

FINANCIAL PLANNER

FOR REDUCING AND MANAGING BILLS

BILLS I AM PAYING OFF

AMOUNT TO PAY OFF

REMINDERS & NOTES

My Personal Planner

TODAY WILL BE EPIC!

DAILY TASKS

_____
_____
_____
_____

THINGS TO DO LOG

☐　　　　　　　　　　☐
☐　　　　　　　　　　☐
☐　　　　　　　　　　☐
☐　　　　　　　　　　☐
☐　　　　　　　　　　☐

NOTES AND REMINDERS

_____
_____
_____
_____

MY MONTHLY FINANCIAL PLANNER

GOALS FOR THE MONTH

- [ ] _____
- [ ] _____
- [ ] _____
- [ ] _____
- [ ] _____
- [ ] _____

DATES TO REMEMBER

IMPORTANT NOTES

- [ ] _____
- [ ] _____
- [ ] _____
- [ ] _____
- [ ] _____
- [ ] _____
- [ ] _____
- [ ] _____
- [ ] _____
- [ ] _____
- [ ] _____

HOW DID YOU DO?
WEEK AT A GLANCE

GOALS:

SHORT TERM

YEARLY

LONG TERM

WORDS TO LIVE BY

NOTES

PRIORITIES

TASKS COMPLETED

ACCOMPLISHMENTS

SAVINGS

(S) (M) (T) (W)
(T) (F) (S)

CHALLENGES

LESSONS LEARNED

The Trusted Banker

Personal Monthly Budget

Projected Monthly Income
Income 1
Extra income
Total monthly income

Projected Balance (Projected income minus expenses)	$
Actual Balance (Actual income minus expenses)	$
Difference (Actual minus projected)	$

Actual Monthly Income	
Income 1	
Extra income	
Total monthly income	

HOUSING	Column 1	Amount Paid	Difference
Mortgage or rent		$	
Phone		$	
Electricity		$	
Gas		$	
Water and sewer		$	
Cable		$	
Waste removal		$	
Maintenance or repairs		$	
Supplies		$	
Other		$	
Subtotal		$	

ENTERTAINMENT	Column 1	Amount Paid	Difference
Video/DVD		$	
CDs		$	
Movies		$	
Concerts		$	
Sporting events		$	
Live theater		$	
Other		$	
Other		$	
Other		$	
Subtotal		$	

TRANSPORTATION	Column 1	Amount Paid	Difference
Vehicle payment		$	
Bus/taxi fare		$	
Insurance		$	
Licensing		$	
Fuel		$	
Maintenance		$	
Other		$	
Subtotal		$	

LOANS	Column 1	Amount Paid	Difference
Personal		$	
Student		$	
Credit card		$	
Credit card		$	
Credit card		$	
Other		$	
Subtotal		$	

INSURANCE	Column1	Amount Paid	Difference
Home		$	
Health		$	
Life		$	
Other		$	
Subtotal		$	

TAXES	Column1	Amount Paid	Difference
Federal		$	
State		$	
Local		$	
Other		$	
Subtotal		$	

FOOD	Column1	Amount Paid	Difference
Groceries		$	
Dining out		$	
Other		$	
Subtotal		$	

SAVINGS OR INVESTMENTS	Column1	Amount Paid	Difference
Retirement account		$	
Investment account		$	
Other		$	
Subtotal		$	

PETS	Column1	Amount Paid	Difference
Food		$	
Medical		$	
Grooming		$	
Toys		$	
Other		$	
Subtotal		$	

WEEKLY SPENDING LOGS	Column1	Amount Paid	Difference
WEEK 1		$	
WEEK 2		$	
WEEK 3		$	
WEEK 4		$	
Subtotal		$	

PERSONAL CARE	Column1	Amount Paid	Difference
Medical		$	
Hair/nails		$	
Clothing		$	
Dry cleaning		$	
Health club		$	
Organization dues or fees		$	
Other		$	
Subtotal		$	

LEGAL	Column1	Amount Paid	Difference
Attorney		$	
Alimony		$	
Payments on lien or judgment		$	
Other		$	
Subtotal		$	

Total Projected Cost	$0.00
Total Actual Cost	$0.00
Total Difference	$0.00

BANKABLE SCHEDULE

DAY 1

DAILY TASKS:
VIEW BANK ACCOUNTS

- Review your Bank Accounts and write down your available balance in each account. You should always be aware of how much money is in your accounts.
- Complete your daily expense log
- Put $1.00 in your challenge envelope

DAILY EXPENSES:

FOOD

TRANSPORTATION

ENTERTAINMENT

GROCERIES

SHOPPING

OTHER

IMPORTANT NOTES:

BANKABLE SCHEDULE

DAY 2

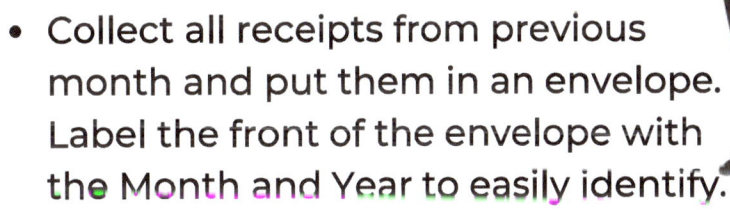

DAILY TASKS: CREATE ENVELOPE FOR PREVIOUS MONTH

- Collect all receipts from previous month and put them in an envelope. Label the front of the envelope with the Month and Year to easily identify.
- Complete your daily expense log.
- Put $2 in your challenge envelope.

DAILY EXPENSES:

FOOD

TRANSPORTATION

ENTERTAINMENT

GROCERIES

SHOPPING

OTHER

IMPORTANT NOTES:

BANKABLE SCHEDULE

DAY 3

DAILY TASKS: MONTHLY GOALS

- Review your goal from last month. Did you reach it? Write down your goal for this month. You can select from the choices on the monthly goal sheet, or create your own.
- Complete your daily expense log.
- Put $3 in your challenge envelope.

DAILY EXPENSES:

FOOD
_____

TRANSPORTATION
_____

ENTERTAINMENT
_____

GROCERIES
_____

SHOPPING
_____

OTHER
_____

IMPORTANT NOTES:

_____
_____
_____
_____
_____

BANKABLE SCHEDULE

DAY 4

DAILY TASKS:
COLLECT SPARE CHANGE

- Review the app Acorn. This app invests money when you make a purchase with your debit/credit card. Purchases are rounded up to the next dollar amount and the change is invested.
- Complete your daily expense log.
- Put $4 in your challenge envelope.

DAILY EXPENSES:

FOOD

TRANSPORTATION

ENTERTAINMENT

GROCERIES

SHOPPING

OTHER

IMPORTANT NOTES:

BANKABLE SCHEDULE

Day 5

DAILY TASKS:
REFLECTION TIME

- Review your receipts from last month and your monthly budget. Did you pay your bills on time? Did you pay anything late?

- Complete your daily expense log.
- Put $5 in your challenge envelope.

DAILY EXPENSES:

FOOD
_____

TRANSPORTATION
_____

ENTERTAINMENT
_____

GROCERIES
_____

SHOPPING
_____

OTHER
_____

IMPORTANT NOTES:

_____
_____
_____
_____

BANKABLE SCHEDULE

Day 6

DAILY TASKS:
WEEKLY RECEIPTS

- Gather all your receipts from the week. Stack them by category (gas, food, shopping, dining, misc) and paper clip them together and place them in the monthly envelope.
- Complete your daily expense log.
- Put $6 in your challenge envelope.

DAILY EXPENSES:

FOOD
_____

TRANSPORTATION
_____

ENTERTAINMENT
_____

GROCERIES
_____

SHOPPING
_____

OTHER
_____

IMPORTANT NOTES:

_____

_____

_____

_____

BANKABLE SCHEDULE

Day 7

DAILY TASKS:
TOTAL SPENDING LOGS

- Total your spending logs from the week and list the total on your master budget in the area labeled "Weekly Spending Log."
- This is week 1.
- Complete your daily expense log.
- Put $7 in your challenge envelope.

DAILY EXPENSES:

FOOD

TRANSPORTATION

ENTERTAINMENT

GROCERIES

SHOPPING

OTHER

IMPORTANT NOTES:

BANKABLE SCHEDULE

DAY 8

DAILY TASKS:
MONTHLY AUTOPAY CHECK-IN

- Confirm: (1) payment are still being deducted as agreed on the correct date. (2) payment has not increased. If you can afford to make an additional payment this month, do it.
- Complete daily expense log.
- Put $8 in your challenge envelope

DAILY EXPENSES:

FOOD
_____

TRANSPORTATION
_____

ENTERTAINMENT
_____

GROCERIES
_____

SHOPPING
_____

OTHER
_____

IMPORTANT NOTES:

_____

_____

_____

_____

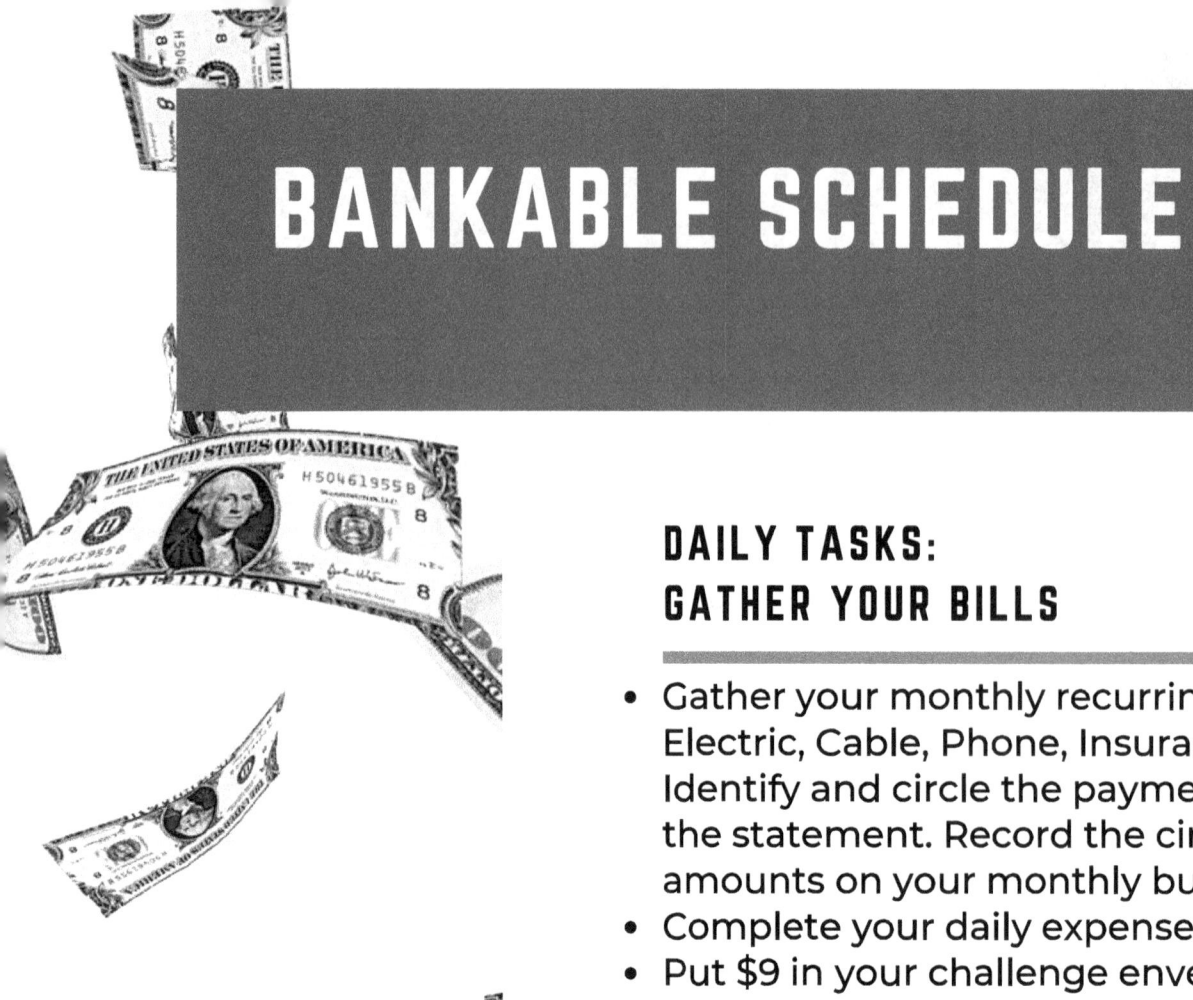

BANKABLE SCHEDULE

Day 9

DAILY TASKS:
GATHER YOUR BILLS

- Gather your monthly recurring bills. Electric, Cable, Phone, Insurance, etc. Identify and circle the payment on the statement. Record the circled amounts on your monthly budget.
- Complete your daily expense log.
- Put $9 in your challenge envelope.

DAILY EXPENSES:

FOOD

TRANSPORTATION

ENTERTAINMENT

GROCERIES

SHOPPING

OTHER

IMPORTANT NOTES:

BANKABLE SCHEDULE

DAY 10

DAILY TASKS:
ONE YEAR GOAL

- Review your one year goal. Is it still something you are passionate about? Do you need to tweak it? Are you on track to achieve it?
- Complete your daily expense log.
- Put $10 in your challenge envelope.

DAILY EXPENSES:

FOOD

TRANSPORTATION

ENTERTAINMENT

GROCERIES

SHOPPING

OTHER

IMPORTANT NOTES:

BANKABLE SCHEDULE

DAY 11

DAILY TASKS: FREE DAY!!!

- Complete your daily expense log.
- Put $11 in your challenge envelope.

DAILY EXPENSES:

FOOD

TRANSPORTATION

ENTERTAINMENT

GROCERIES

SHOPPING

OTHER

IMPORTANT NOTES:

BANKABLE SCHEDULE

Day 12

DAILY TASKS: PLAN TODAY TO RAISE YOUR LIMIT

- Read your free credit report. Verify your name, address, date of birth and social security number are accurate and spelled correctly.
- Complete your daily expense log.
- Put $12 in your challenge envelope.

DAILY EXPENSES:

FOOD
_____

TRANSPORTATION
_____

ENTERTAINMENT
_____

GROCERIES
_____

SHOPPING
_____

OTHER
_____

IMPORTANT NOTES:

_____
_____
_____
_____

BANKABLE SCHEDULE

DAY 13

DAILY TASKS:
GATHER YOUR RECEIPTS

- Categorize all your receipts for the week (gas, food, shopping, dining, misc.) paper clip them together to place in your monthly envelope.
- Complete your daily expense log.
- Put $13 in your challenge envelope.

DAILY EXPENSES:

FOOD

TRANSPORTATION

ENTERTAINMENT

GROCERIES

SHOPPING

OTHER

IMPORTANT NOTES:

BANKABLE SCHEDULE

DAY 14

DAILY TASKS:
TOTAL SPENDING LOGS

- Total your spending logs from the week and list the total on your master budget in the area labeled "Weekly Spending Log."
- This is week 2.
- Complete your daily expense log.
- Put $14 in your challenge envelope.

DAILY EXPENSES:

FOOD

TRANSPORTATION

ENTERTAINMENT

GROCERIES

SHOPPING

OTHER

IMPORTANT NOTES:

BANKABLE SCHEDULE

DAY 15

DAILY TASKS:
HALF WAY POINT

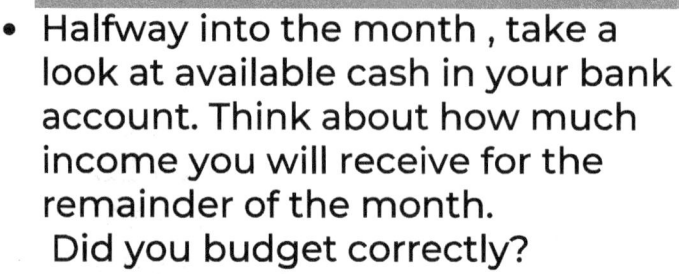

- Halfway into the month, take a look at available cash in your bank account. Think about how much income you will receive for the remainder of the month. Did you budget correctly?
- Complete daily expense log.
- Put $15 in your challenge envelope.

DAILY EXPENSES:

FOOD

TRANSPORTATION

ENTERTAINMENT

GROCERIES

SHOPPING

OTHER

IMPORTANT NOTES:

BANKABLE SCHEDULE

DAY 16

DAILY TASKS:
REDUCE MONTHLY DEBT

- Check out free apps: Truebill, Mint, Trim or Bobby. These apps help you identify and manage recurring bills. For more information refer to the page titled "4 Free Apps".
- Complete your daily expense log.
- Put $16 in your challenge envelope.

DAILY EXPENSES:

FOOD

TRANSPORTATION

ENTERTAINMENT

GROCERIES

SHOPPING

OTHER

IMPORTANT NOTES:

BANKABLE SCHEDULE

DAY 17

DAILY TASKS:
LONG TERM GOAL

- Review your Long Term Goal. Create a plan of action to achieve your goal. Create a time line of multiple benchmarks that will lead you to your goal.
- Complete daily expense log.
- Put $17 in your challenge envelope.

DAILY EXPENSES:

FOOD

TRANSPORTATION

ENTERTAINMENT

GROCERIES

SHOPPING

OTHER

IMPORTANT NOTES:

BANKABLE SCHEDULE

DAY 18

DAILY TASKS:
GATHER SPARE CHANGE

- Empty the spare change out of your pockets, purse, car and coats. Think of other places you may have spare change. Gather it and put it in a jar. Label the jar "My Savings Jar"
- Complete your daily expense log.
- Put 18 in your challenge envelope.

DAILY EXPENSES:

FOOD

TRANSPORTATION

ENTERTAINMENT

GROCERIES

SHOPPING

OTHER

IMPORTANT NOTES:

BANKABLE SCHEDULE

DAY 19

DAILY TASKS: MONTHLY PAYMENT PLAN CHECK-IN

- Confirm payment have been deducted for the accounts you made payment arrangement for last month. Make an extra payment to reduce your balance even more.
- Complete your daily expense log.
- Put $19 in your challenge envelope.

DAILY EXPENSES:

FOOD

TRANSPORTATION

ENTERTAINMENT

GROCERIES

SHOPPING

OTHER

IMPORTANT NOTES:

BANKABLE SCHEDULE

DAY 20

DAILY TASKS:
GATHER YOUR RECEIPTS

- Categorize all your receipts for the week (gas, food, shopping, dining, misc.) paper clip them together to place in your monthly envelope.
- Complete your daily expense log.
- Put $20 in your challenge envelope.

DAILY EXPENSES:

FOOD

TRANSPORTATION

ENTERTAINMENT

GROCERIES

SHOPPING

OTHER

IMPORTANT NOTES:

BANKABLE SCHEDULE

DAY 21

DAILY TASKS:
TOTAL SPENDING LOGS

- Total your spending logs from the week and list the total on your master budget in the area labeled "Weekly Spending Log."
- This is week 3.
- Complete your daily expense log.
- Put $21 in your challenge envelope.

DAILY EXPENSES:

FOOD

TRANSPORTATION

ENTERTAINMENT

GROCERIES

SHOPPING

OTHER

IMPORTANT NOTES:

BANKABLE SCHEDULE

DAY 22

DAILY TASKS:
REVIEW BANK STATEMENT

- Review your bank statement. On your master budget, log the date each recurring bills is deducted. Check monthly service charges to ensure no overcharging of fees.
- Complete your daily expense log.
- Put $22 in your challenge envelope.

DAILY EXPENSES:

FOOD

TRANSPORTATION

ENTERTAINMENT

GROCERIES

SHOPPING

OTHER

IMPORTANT NOTES:

BANKABLE SCHEDULE

DAY 23

DAILY TASKS:
REDUCE MONTHLY DEBT

- Select a monthly service provider and ask if they have any specials to lower your bill. If not, tell them you are shopping around to get the best rate.
- Complete your daily expense log.
- Put $23 in your challenge envelope.

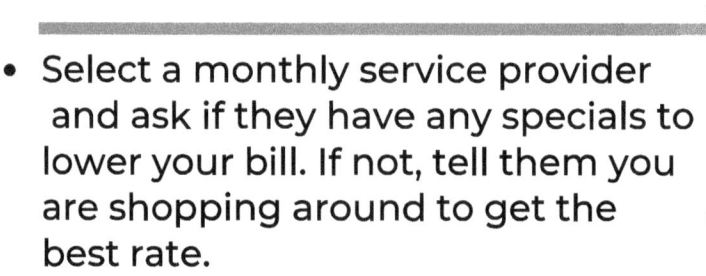

DAILY EXPENSES:

FOOD

TRANSPORTATION

ENTERTAINMENT

GROCERIES

SHOPPING

OTHER

IMPORTANT NOTES:

BANKABLE SCHEDULE

DAY 24

DAILY TASKS:
MANAGE COLLECTION ACCOUNTS

- Now that you have paid on your collection accounts and arranged a manageable payment arrangement, determine if you can afford to pay off an account In full.
- Complete your daily expense log.
- Put $24 in your challenge envelope.

DAILY EXPENSES:

FOOD

TRANSPORTATION

ENTERTAINMENT

GROCERIES

SHOPPING

OTHER

IMPORTANT NOTES:

BANKABLE SCHEDULE

DAY 25

DAILY TASKS: FREE DAY!!!

- Complete your daily expense log.
- Put $25 in your challenge envelope.

DAILY EXPENSES:

FOOD

TRANSPORTATION

ENTERTAINMENT

GROCERIES

SHOPPING

OTHER

IMPORTANT NOTES:

BANKABLE SCHEDULE

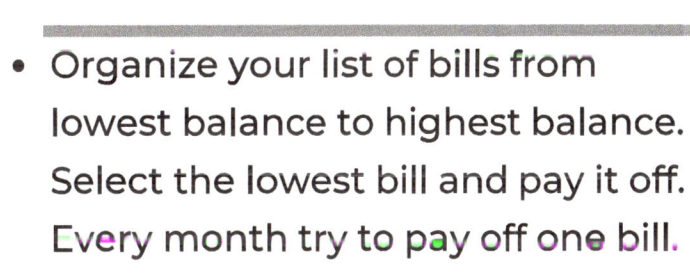

DAY 26

DAILY TASKS:
PAY-OFF YOUR BILLS

- Organize your list of bills from lowest balance to highest balance. Select the lowest bill and pay it off. Every month try to pay off one bill.
- Complete your daily expense log.
- Put $26 in your challenge envelope.

DAILY EXPENSES:

FOOD

TRANSPORTATION

ENTERTAINMENT

GROCERIES

SHOPPING

OTHER

IMPORTANT NOTES:

BANKABLE SCHEDULE

DAY 27

DAILY TASKS:
GATHER YOUR RECEIPTS

- Categorize all your receipts for the week (gas, food, shopping, dining, misc.) paper clip them together to place in your monthly envelope.
- Complete your daily expense log.
- Put $27 in your challenge envelope.

DAILY EXPENSES:

FOOD

TRANSPORTATION

ENTERTAINMENT

GROCERIES

SHOPPING

OTHER

IMPORTANT NOTES:

BANKABLE SCHEDULE

DAY 28

DAILY TASKS:
TOTAL SPENDING LOGS

- Total your spending logs from the week and list the total on your master budget in the area labeled "Weekly Spending Log."
- This is week 4.
- Complete your daily expense log.
- Put $28 in your challenge envelope.

DAILY EXPENSES:

FOOD

TRANSPORTATION

ENTERTAINMENT

GROCERIES

SHOPPING

OTHER

IMPORTANT NOTES:

BANKABLE SCHEDULE

Day 29

DAILY TASKS:
MAKE ADDITIONAL INCOME

- Identify ways you can make additional income. What are your hobbies? What do you like to do and what are you good at? What is your passion?
- Complete your daily expense log.
- Put $29 in your challenge envelope

DAILY EXPENSES:

FOOD

TRANSPORTATION

ENTERTAINMENT

GROCERIES

SHOPPING

OTHER

IMPORTANT NOTES:

BANKABLE SCHEDULE

DAY 30

DAILY TASKS:
GATHER SPARE CHANGE

- Every month you will be surprised with the amount of spare change you can find laying around. Collect it all and put it in your "Savings Jar".
- Complete your daily expense log.
- Put $30 in your challenge envelope.

DAILY EXPENSES:

FOOD
_____

TRANSPORTATION
_____

ENTERTAINMENT
_____

GROCERIES
_____

SHOPPING
_____

OTHER
_____

IMPORTANT NOTES:

_____
_____
_____
_____

BANKABLE SCHEDULE

DAY 31

DAILY TASKS: FREE DAY!!!

- Complete your daily expense log.
- Put $31 in your challenge envelope.

DAILY EXPENSES:

FOOD

TRANSPORTATION

ENTERTAINMENT

GROCERIES

SHOPPING

OTHER

IMPORTANT NOTES:

_____,20
    month   day   year

MY DAILY PLANNER

THINGS TO DO

MY CONTACT LOG

REMINDERS & NOTES

The Trusted Banker

WEEKLY MONEY LOGS

MONDAY

TUESDAY

WEDNESDAY

THURSDAY

FRIDAY

SATURDAY

NOTES

The Trusted Banker

Bankable Planner
Short Term Goal Planner

SHORT TERM GOALS

Short Term Goals I'm Interested In

- [ ] _____
- [ ] _____
- [ ] _____
- [ ] _____
- [ ] _____
- [ ] _____
- [ ] _____

Notes to Self

_____

_____

_____

_____

_____

Bankable Planner
Yearly Goal Planner

YEARLY GOALS

Yearly Goals I'm Interested In

- [ ] _____
- [ ] _____
- [ ] _____
- [ ] _____
- [ ] _____
- [ ] _____
- [ ] _____

Notes to Self

_____
_____
_____
_____
_____

Bankable Planner
Long Term Goal Planner

LONG TERM GOALS

LONG TERM GOALS I'M INTERESTED IN

- [ ] _____
- [ ] _____
- [ ] _____
- [ ] _____
- [ ] _____
- [ ] _____
- [ ] _____

NOTES TO SELF

_____
_____
_____
_____
_____
_____

The Trusted Banker

FINANCIAL PLANNER
FOR REDUCING AND MANAGING BILLS

BILLS I AM PAYING OFF

AMOUNT TO PAY OFF

REMINDERS & NOTES

My Personal Planner

TODAY WILL BE EPIC!

DAILY TASKS

_____
_____
_____
_____

THINGS TO DO LOG

- [ ]
- [ ]
- [ ]
- [ ]
- [ ]

- [ ]
- [ ]
- [ ]
- [ ]
- [ ]

NOTES AND REMINDERS

_____
_____
_____
_____

MY MONTHLY FINANCIAL PLANNER

GOALS FOR THE MONTH

- [ ] _____
- [ ] _____
- [ ] _____
- [ ] _____
- [ ] _____
- [ ] _____

DATES TO REMEMBER

IMPORTANT NOTES

- [ ] _____
- [ ] _____
- [ ] _____
- [ ] _____
- [ ] _____
- [ ] _____
- [ ] _____
- [ ] _____
- [ ] _____
- [ ] _____
- [ ] _____
- [ ] _____

HOW DID YOU DO?
WEEK AT A GLANCE

GOALS:

SHORT TERM

YEARLY

LONG TERM

WORDS TO LIVE BY

NOTES

PRIORITIES

TASKS COMPLETED

ACCOMPLISHMENTS

SAVINGS

(S) (M) (T) (W)
(T) (F) (S)

CHALLENGES

LESSONS LEARNED

The Trusted Banker

Personal Monthly Budget

Projected Monthly Income	
Income 1	
Extra income	
Total monthly income	

Actual Monthly Income	
Income 1	
Extra income	
Total monthly income	

Projected Balance (Projected income minus expenses)	$
Actual Balance (Actual income minus expenses)	$
Difference (Actual minus projected)	$

HOUSING	Column 1	Amount Paid	Difference
Mortgage or rent		$	
Phone		$	
Electricity		$	
Gas		$	
Water and sewer		$	
Cable		$	
Waste removal		$	
Maintenance or repairs		$	
Supplies		$	
Other		$	
Subtotal		$	

ENTERTAINMENT	Column 1	Amount Paid	Difference
Video/DVD		$	
CDs		$	
Movies		$	
Concerts		$	
Sporting events		$	
Live theater		$	
Other		$	
Other		$	
Other		$	
Subtotal		$	

TRANSPORTATION	Column 1	Amount Paid	Difference
Vehicle payment		$	
Bus/taxi fare		$	
Insurance		$	
Licensing		$	
Fuel		$	
Maintenance		$	
Other		$	
Subtotal		$	

LOANS	Column 1	Amount Paid	Difference
Personal		$	
Student		$	
Credit card		$	
Credit card		$	
Credit card		$	
Other		$	
Subtotal		$	

INSURANCE	Column1	Amount Paid	Difference
Home		$	
Health		$	
Life		$	
Other		$	
Subtotal		$	

TAXES	Column1	Amount Paid	Difference
Federal		$	
State		$	
Local		$	
Other		$	
Subtotal		$	

FOOD	Column1	Amount Paid	Difference
Groceries		$	
Dining out		$	
Other		$	
Subtotal		$	

SAVINGS OR INVESTMENTS	Column1	Amount Paid	Difference
Retirement account		$	
Investment account		$	
Other		$	
Subtotal		$	

PETS	Column1	Amount Paid	Difference
Food		$	
Medical		$	
Grooming		$	
Toys		$	
Other		$	
Subtotal		$	

WEEKLY SPENDING LOGS	Column1	Amount Paid	Difference
WEEK 1		$	
WEEK 2		$	
WEEK 3		$	
WEEK 4		$	
Subtotal		$	

PERSONAL CARE	Column1	Amount Paid	Difference
Medical		$	
Hair/nails		$	
Clothing		$	
Dry cleaning		$	
Health club		$	
Organization dues or fees		$	
Other		$	
Subtotal		$	

LEGAL	Column1	Amount Paid	Difference
Attorney		$	
Alimony		$	
Payments on lien or judgment		$	
Other		$	
Subtotal		$	

Total Projected Cost	$0.00
Total Actual Cost	$0.00
Total Difference	$0.00

BANKABLE SCHEDULE

Day 1

DAILY TASKS:
VIEW BANK ACCOUNTS

- Review your Bank Accounts and write down your available balance in each account. Every month document your liquid balance on the first of the month.
- Complete your daily expense log
- Put $1.00 in your challenge envelope

DAILY EXPENSES:

FOOD
_____

TRANSPORTATION
_____

ENTERTAINMENT
_____

GROCERIES
_____

SHOPPING
_____

OTHER
_____

IMPORTANT NOTES:

_____

_____

_____

_____

BANKABLE SCHEDULE

Day 2

DAILY TASKS: CREATE ENVELOPE FOR PREVIOUS MONTH

- Collect all receipts from previous month and put them in an envelope. Label the front of the envelope with the Month and Year to easily identify.
- Complete your daily expense log.
- Put $2 in your challenge envelope.

DAILY EXPENSES:

FOOD
___

TRANSPORTATION
___

ENTERTAINMENT
___

GROCERIES
___

SHOPPING
___

OTHER
___

IMPORTANT NOTES:

___
___
___
___
___

BANKABLE SCHEDULE

DAY 3

DAILY TASKS:
MONTHLY GOALS

- Review your goal from last month. Did you reach it? Write down your goal for this month. You can select from the choices on the monthly goal sheet, or create your own.
- Complete your daily expense log.
- Put $3 in your challenge envelope.

DAILY EXPENSES:

FOOD
_____

TRANSPORTATION
_____

ENTERTAINMENT
_____

GROCERIES
_____

SHOPPING
_____

OTHER
_____

IMPORTANT NOTES:

_____

_____

_____

_____

BANKABLE SCHEDULE

Day 4

DAILY TASKS:
COLLECT SPARE CHANGE

- Review the app "Digit". This app creates savings goals, manages debts, and automatically saves a little bit of money each day based on your spending habits.
- Complete your daily expense log.
- Put $4 in your challenge envelope.

DAILY EXPENSES:

FOOD
_____

TRANSPORTATION
_____

ENTERTAINMENT
_____

GROCERIES
_____

SHOPPING
_____

OTHER
_____

IMPORTANT NOTES:
_____
_____
_____
_____
_____

BANKABLE SCHEDULE

DAY 5

DAILY TASKS:
REFLECTION TIME

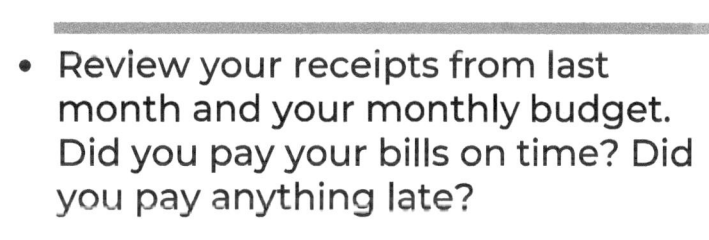

- Review your receipts from last month and your monthly budget. Did you pay your bills on time? Did you pay anything late?

- Complete your daily expense log.
- Put $5 in your challenge envelope.

DAILY EXPENSES:

FOOD
_____

TRANSPORTATION
_____

ENTERTAINMENT
_____

GROCERIES
_____

SHOPPING
_____

OTHER
_____

IMPORTANT NOTES:

_____

_____

_____

_____

BANKABLE SCHEDULE

Day 6

DAILY TASKS: WEEKLY RECEIPTS

- Gather all your receipts from the week. Stack them by category (gas, food, shopping, dining, misc) and paper clip them together and place them in the monthly envelope.
- Complete your daily expense log.
- Put $6 in your challenge envelope.

DAILY EXPENSES:

FOOD
_____

TRANSPORTATION
_____

ENTERTAINMENT
_____

GROCERIES
_____

SHOPPING
_____

OTHER
_____

IMPORTANT NOTES:

_____
_____
_____
_____

BANKABLE SCHEDULE

DAY 7

DAILY TASKS:
TOTAL SPENDING LOGS

- Total your spending logs from the week and list the total on your master budget in the area labeled "Weekly Spending Log."
- This is week 1.
- Complete your daily expense log.
- Put $7 in your challenge envelope.

DAILY EXPENSES:

FOOD
_____

TRANSPORTATION
_____

ENTERTAINMENT
_____

GROCERIES
_____

SHOPPING
_____

OTHER
_____

IMPORTANT NOTES:
_____
_____
_____
_____
_____

BANKABLE SCHEDULE

Day 8

DAILY TASKS:
MONTHLY AUTOPAY CHECK-IN

- Confirm: (1) payment are still being deducted as agreed on the correct date. (2) payment has not increased. If you can afford to make an additional payment this month, do it.
- Complete daily expense log.
- Put $8 in your challenge envelope

DAILY EXPENSES:

FOOD

TRANSPORTATION

ENTERTAINMENT

GROCERIES

SHOPPING

OTHER

IMPORTANT NOTES:

BANKABLE SCHEDULE

DAY 9

DAILY TASKS:
GATHER YOUR BILLS

- Gather your monthly recurring bills. Electric, Cable, Phone, Insurance, etc. Identify and circle the payment on the statement. Record the circled amounts on your monthly budget.
- Complete your daily expense log.
- Put $9 in your challenge envelope.

DAILY EXPENSES:

FOOD

TRANSPORTATION

ENTERTAINMENT

GROCERIES

SHOPPING

OTHER

IMPORTANT NOTES:

BANKABLE SCHEDULE

DAY 10

DAILY TASKS:
ONE YEAR GOAL

- Review your one year goal. Are you on track to reach your goal? Do you need to enroll in classes, get certified, purchase any licenses. Using your timeline, create a "To Do" list.
- Complete your daily expense log.
- Put $10 in your challenge envelope.

DAILY EXPENSES:

FOOD

TRANSPORTATION

ENTERTAINMENT

GROCERIES

SHOPPING

OTHER

IMPORTANT NOTES:

BANKABLE SCHEDULE

DAY 11

DAILY TASKS: FREE DAY!!!

- Complete your daily expense log.
- Put $11 in your challenge envelope.

DAILY EXPENSES:

FOOD

TRANSPORTATION

ENTERTAINMENT

GROCERIES

SHOPPING

OTHER

IMPORTANT NOTES:

BANKABLE SCHEDULE

DAY 12

DAILY TASKS: PLAN TODAY TO RAISE YOUR LIMIT

- Start paying a credit card 2 days before the due date for six months. The seventh month ask to increase your credit limit. But don't use it.
- Complete your daily expense log.
- Put $12 in your challenge envelope.

DAILY EXPENSES:

FOOD

TRANSPORTATION

ENTERTAINMENT

GROCERIES

SHOPPING

OTHER

IMPORTANT NOTES:

BANKABLE SCHEDULE

DAY 13

DAILY TASKS:
GATHER YOUR RECEIPTS

- Categorize all your receipts for the week (gas, food, shopping, dining, misc.) paper clip them together to place in your monthly envelope.
- Complete your daily expense log.
- Put $13 in your challenge envelope.

DAILY EXPENSES:

FOOD

TRANSPORTATION

ENTERTAINMENT

GROCERIES

SHOPPING

OTHER

IMPORTANT NOTES:

BANKABLE SCHEDULE

DAY 14

DAILY TASKS:
TOTAL SPENDING LOGS

- Total your spending logs from the week and list the total on your master budget in the area labeled "Weekly Spending Log."
- This is week 2.
- Complete your daily expense log.
- Put $14 in your challenge envelope.

DAILY EXPENSES:

FOOD

TRANSPORTATION

ENTERTAINMENT

GROCERIES

SHOPPING

OTHER

IMPORTANT NOTES:

BANKABLE SCHEDULE

DAY 15

DAILY TASKS:
HALF WAY POINT

- Halfway into the month, take a look at available cash in your bank account. Think about how much income you will receive for the remainder of the month. Did you budget correctly?
- Complete daily expense log.
- Put $15 in your challenge envelope.

DAILY EXPENSES:

FOOD

TRANSPORTATION

ENTERTAINMENT

GROCERIES

SHOPPING

OTHER

IMPORTANT NOTES:

BANKABLE SCHEDULE

DAY 16

DAILY TASKS:
DOUBLE UP ON PAYMENTS

- If you paid off bills in the last two months, choose a bill and double up on the payment to reduce your balance quicker.
- Complete your daily expense log.
- Put $16 in your challenge envelope.

DAILY EXPENSES:

FOOD

TRANSPORTATION

ENTERTAINMENT

GROCERIES

SHOPPING

OTHER

IMPORTANT NOTES:

BANKABLE SCHEDULE

DAY 17

DAILY TASKS:
LONG TERM GOAL

- Review your Long Term Goal. Start putting money aside to save for your long term goal. Create a visual so you can view your long term goal. If you can see it, you can achieve it.
- Complete daily expense log.
- Put $17 in your challenge envelope.

DAILY EXPENSES:

FOOD

TRANSPORTATION

ENTERTAINMENT

GROCERIES

SHOPPING

OTHER

IMPORTANT NOTES:

BANKABLE SCHEDULE

DAY 18

DAILY TASKS:
GATHER SPARE CHANGE

- Empty the spare change out of your pockets, purse, car and coats. Think of other places you may have spare change. Gather it and put it in a jar. Label the jar "My Savings Jar"
- Complete your daily expense log.
- Put 18 in your challenge envelope.

DAILY EXPENSES:

FOOD

TRANSPORTATION

ENTERTAINMENT

GROCERIES

SHOPPING

OTHER

IMPORTANT NOTES:

BANKABLE SCHEDULE

DAY 19

DAILY TASKS: MONTHLY PAYMENT PLAN CHECK-IN

- Confirm payment have been deducted for the accounts you made payment arrangement for last month. Make an extra payment to reduce your balance even more.
- Complete your daily expense log.
- Put $19 in your challenge envelope.

DAILY EXPENSES:

FOOD
_____

TRANSPORTATION
_____

ENTERTAINMENT
_____

GROCERIES
_____

SHOPPING
_____

OTHER
_____

IMPORTANT NOTES:

_____
_____
_____
_____

BANKABLE SCHEDULE

DAY 20

DAILY TASKS:
GATHER YOUR RECEIPTS

- Categorize all your receipts for the week (gas, food, shopping, dining, misc.) paper clip them together to place in your monthly envelope.
- Complete your daily expense log.
- Put $20 in your challenge envelope.

DAILY EXPENSES:

FOOD
___

TRANSPORTATION
___

ENTERTAINMENT
___

GROCERIES
___

SHOPPING
___

OTHER
___

IMPORTANT NOTES:
___
___
___
___
___

BANKABLE SCHEDULE

DAY 21

DAILY TASKS:
TOTAL SPENDING LOGS

- Total your spending logs from the week and list the total on your master budget in the area labeled "Weekly Spending Log."
- This is week 3.
- Complete your daily expense log.
- Put $21 in your challenge envelope.

DAILY EXPENSES:

FOOD

TRANSPORTATION

ENTERTAINMENT

GROCERIES

SHOPPING

OTHER

IMPORTANT NOTES:

BANKABLE SCHEDULE

DAY 22

DAILY TASKS:
REVIEW BANK STATEMENT

- Review your bank statement. On your master budget, log the date each recurring bills is deducted. Check monthly service charges to ensure no overcharging of fees.
- Complete your daily expense log.
- Put $22 in your challenge envelope.

DAILY EXPENSES:

FOOD

TRANSPORTATION

ENTERTAINMENT

GROCERIES

SHOPPING

OTHER

IMPORTANT NOTES:

BANKABLE SCHEDULE

DAY 23

DAILY TASKS:
LOOK FOR INVESTMENTS

- Explore investing in stocks, real estate, new business ventures, mutual funds, life insurance etc. Get advicebanker, financial planner and insurance agent.
- Complete your daily expense log.
- Put $23 in your challenge envelope.

DAILY EXPENSES:

FOOD

TRANSPORTATION

ENTERTAINMENT

GROCERIES

SHOPPING

OTHER

IMPORTANT NOTES:

BANKABLE SCHEDULE

Day 24

DAILY TASKS:
VERIFIED COLLECTION PAY-OFFS

- For every collection account you pay off, call the collection company and ask them to mail you a letter saying collection account is paid in full. Keep for your records.
- Complete your daily expense log.
- Put $24 in your challenge envelope.

DAILY EXPENSES:

FOOD

TRANSPORTATION

ENTERTAINMENT

GROCERIES

SHOPPING

OTHER

IMPORTANT NOTES:

BANKABLE SCHEDULE

Day 25

DAILY TASKS: FREE DAY!!!

- Complete your daily expense log.
- Put $25 in your challenge envelope.

DAILY EXPENSES:

FOOD

TRANSPORTATION

ENTERTAINMENT

GROCERIES

SHOPPING

OTHER

IMPORTANT NOTES:

BANKABLE SCHEDULE

DAY 26

DAILY TASKS:
PAY-OFF YOUR BILLS

- Continue to pay off your bills on the list you created last month. Every month try to pay off one bill until they are all paid off.
- Complete your daily expense log.
- Put $26 in your challenge envelope.

DAILY EXPENSES:

FOOD

TRANSPORTATION

ENTERTAINMENT

GROCERIES

SHOPPING

OTHER

IMPORTANT NOTES:

BANKABLE SCHEDULE

DAY 27

DAILY TASKS:
GATHER YOUR RECEIPTS

- Categorize all your receipts for the week (gas, food, shopping, dining, misc.) paper clip them together to place in your monthly envelope.
- Complete your daily expense log.
- Put $27 in your challenge envelope.

DAILY EXPENSES:

FOOD

TRANSPORTATION

ENTERTAINMENT

GROCERIES

SHOPPING

OTHER

IMPORTANT NOTES:

BANKABLE SCHEDULE

DAY 28

DAILY TASKS:
TOTAL SPENDING LOGS

- Total your spending logs from the week and list the total on your master budget in the area labeled "Weekly Spending Log."
- This is week 4.
- Complete your daily expense log.
- Put $28 in your challenge envelope.

DAILY EXPENSES:

FOOD

TRANSPORTATION

ENTERTAINMENT

GROCERIES

SHOPPING

OTHER

IMPORTANT NOTES:

BANKABLE SCHEDULE

Day 29

DAILY TASKS:
MAKE ADDITIONAL INCOME

- Write out a plan to monetize the ideas you wrote down last month. Challenge yourself to create an extra income with low start up costs.
- Complete your daily expense log.
- Put $29 in your challenge envelope

DAILY EXPENSES:

FOOD

TRANSPORTATION

ENTERTAINMENT

GROCERIES

SHOPPING

OTHER

IMPORTANT NOTES:

BANKABLE SCHEDULE

DAY 30

DAILY TASKS:
GATHER SPARE CHANGE

- Every month you will be surprised with the amount of spare change you can find laying around. Collect it all and put it in your "Savings Jar".
- Complete your daily expense log.
- Put $30 in your challenge envelope.

DAILY EXPENSES:

FOOD

TRANSPORTATION

ENTERTAINMENT

GROCERIES

SHOPPING

OTHER

IMPORTANT NOTES:

BANKABLE SCHEDULE

Day 31

DAILY TASKS: FREE DAY!!!

- Complete your daily expense log.
- Put $31 in your challenge envelope.

DAILY EXPENSES:

FOOD

TRANSPORTATION

ENTERTAINMENT

GROCERIES

SHOPPING

OTHER

IMPORTANT NOTES:

_____ _____ ,20
month　　day　　year

MY DAILY PLANNER

THINGS TO DO

MY CONTACT LOG

REMINDERS & NOTES

The Trusted Banker

WEEKLY MONEY LOGS

MONDAY

TUESDAY

WEDNESDAY

THURSDAY

FRIDAY

SATURDAY

NOTES

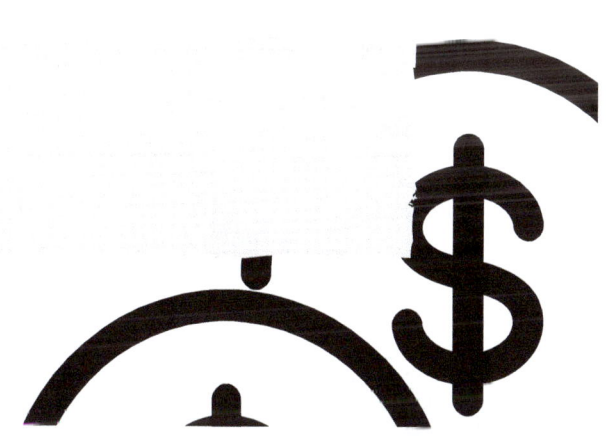

The Trusted Banker

BANKABLE PLANNER
SHORT TERM GOAL PLANNER

SHORT TERM GOALS

SHORT TERM GOALS I'M INTERESTED IN

- [ ] _____
- [ ] _____
- [ ] _____
- [ ] _____
- [ ] _____
- [ ] _____
- [ ] _____

NOTES TO SELF

_____

_____

_____

_____

_____

Bankable Planner
Yearly Goal Planner

YEARLY GOALS

Yearly Goals I'm Interested In

- [ ] _____
- [ ] _____
- [ ] _____
- [ ] _____
- [ ] _____
- [ ] _____
- [ ] _____

Notes to Self

_____

_____

_____

_____

_____

Bankable Planner
Long Term Goal Planner

LONG TERM GOALS

Long Term Goals I'm Interested In

- ☐ _____
- ☐ _____
- ☐ _____
- ☐ _____
- ☐ _____
- ☐ _____
- ☐ _____

Notes to Self

_____

_____

_____

_____

_____

The Trusted Banker

FINANCIAL PLANNER
FOR REDUCING AND MANAGING BILLS

BILLS I AM PAYING OFF

AMOUNT TO PAY OFF

REMINDERS & NOTES

My Personal Planner

TODAY WILL BE EPIC!

DAILY TASKS

_____
_____
_____
_____

THINGS TO DO LOG

☐　　　　　　　　　☐
☐　　　　　　　　　☐
☐　　　　　　　　　☐
☐　　　　　　　　　☐
☐　　　　　　　　　☐

NOTES AND REMINDERS

_____
_____
_____
_____

MY MONTHLY FINANCIAL PLANNER

GOALS FOR THE MONTH

- [ ] _____
- [ ] _____
- [ ] _____
- [ ] _____
- [ ] _____
- [ ] _____

DATES TO REMEMBER

IMPORTANT NOTES

- [ ] _____
- [ ] _____
- [ ] _____
- [ ] _____
- [ ] _____
- [ ] _____
- [ ] _____
- [ ] _____
- [ ] _____
- [ ] _____
- [ ] _____
- [ ] _____

HOW DID YOU DO?
WEEK AT A GLANCE

GOALS:

SHORT TERM

YEARLY

LONG TERM

WORDS TO LIVE BY

NOTES

PRIORITIES

TASKS COMPLETED

ACCOMPLISHMENTS

SAVINGS

(S) (M) (T) (W)
(T) (F) (S)

CHALLENGES

LESSONS LEARNED

The Trusted Banker

Personal Monthly Budget

Projected Monthly Income
Income 1
Extra income
Total monthly income

Actual Monthly Income	
Income 1	
Extra income	
Total monthly income	

Projected Balance (Projected income minus expenses)	$
Actual Balance (Actual income minus expenses)	$
Difference (Actual minus projected)	$

HOUSING	Column 1	Amount Paid	Difference
Mortgage or rent		$	
Phone		$	
Electricity		$	
Gas		$	
Water and sewer		$	
Cable		$	
Waste removal		$	
Maintenance or repairs		$	
Supplies		$	
Other		$	
Subtotal		$	

ENTERTAINMENT	Column 1	Amount Paid	Difference
Video/DVD		$	
CDs		$	
Movies		$	
Concerts		$	
Sporting events		$	
Live theater		$	
Other		$	
Other		$	
Other		$	
Subtotal		$	

TRANSPORTATION	Column 1	Amount Paid	Difference
Vehicle payment		$	
Bus/taxi fare		$	
Insurance		$	
Licensing		$	
Fuel		$	
Maintenance		$	
Other		$	
Subtotal		$	

LOANS	Column 1	Amount Paid	Difference
Personal		$	
Student		$	
Credit card		$	
Credit card		$	
Credit card		$	
Other		$	
Subtotal		$	

INSURANCE	Column1	Amount Paid	Difference
Home		$	
Health		$	
Life		$	
Other		$	
Subtotal		$	

TAXES	Column1	Amount Paid	Difference
Federal		$	
State		$	
Local		$	
Other		$	
Subtotal		$	

FOOD	Column1	Amount Paid	Difference
Groceries		$	
Dining out		$	
Other		$	
Subtotal		$	

SAVINGS OR INVESTMENTS	Column1	Amount Paid	Difference
Retirement account		$	
Investment account		$	
Other		$	
Subtotal		$	

PETS	Column1	Amount Paid	Difference
Food		$	
Medical		$	
Grooming		$	
Toys		$	
Other		$	
Subtotal		$	

WEEKLY SPENDING LOGS	Column1	Amount Paid	Difference
WEEK 1		$	
WEEK 2		$	
WEEK 3		$	
WEEK 4		$	
Subtotal		$	

PERSONAL CARE	Column1	Amount Paid	Difference
Medical		$	
Hair/nails		$	
Clothing		$	
Dry cleaning		$	
Health club		$	
Organization dues or fees		$	
Other		$	
Subtotal		$	

LEGAL	Column1	Amount Paid	Difference
Attorney		$	
Alimony		$	
Payments on lien or judgment		$	
Other		$	
Subtotal		$	

Total Projected Cost	$0.00
Total Actual Cost	$0.00
Total Difference	$0.00

About The Author

Lysa Davis
is
The Trusted Banker

Lysa is the CEO and founder of Community-Up a nonprofit with the social impact mission to eradicate poverty through systemic transformation within low-income communities. Lysa oversaw the fund development and program development work, and spearheaded the nationally recognized **Community-Up Community Development Conference**. For over fifteen years, Lysa has previously served as a Mortgage Manager and Community Reinvestment Officer with several banking institutions, pioneering affordable housing and economic development initiatives in Michigan, Ohio, Indiana and Illinois.

She is most proud of her work that leveraged over $30 million in Department of Justice and Federal Home Loan Bank of Indianapolis resources to create hundreds of units of affordable housing, real estate developments and provide home improvements to low-income communities.

In 2016 Lysa retired from banking after 20 years, and started her own consulting firm, Compliance and Community Consultants, LLC, providing business leaders with a forward-thinking team of experts committed to providing people-centered, results-focused solutions to meet your business challenges and organizational needs.

In doing this work, Lysa created a niche on social media through her web series, **The Trusted Banker**, launching the Financial Fitness challenge, encouraging brick and mortar business to move online, helping entrepreneurs uncover and monetize their gifts on social media and helping 1 million people "Become Bankable"

As a native Detroiter, Lysa graduated from Wayne State University with a BA in Sociology. Lysa currently resides in Detroit with her two daughters and Corey their Maltipoo.

For more information about The Trusted Banker please visit the website www.thetrustedbanker.com

CPSIA information can be obtained
at www.ICGtesting.com
Printed in the USA
LVHW020750160322
713569LV00008B/710

9 781716 825873